Who Was Bob Marley?

by Katie Ellison

illustrated by Gregory Copeland

Penguin Workshop

For all my teachers and students, and a very special thank-you to Guy Cunningham—KE

To my brother, Dr. Rick, to whom I'm indebted —GC

PENGUIN WORKSHOP
An Imprint of Penguin Random House LLC, New York

Published by Penguin Workshop, an imprint of Penguin Random House LLC, New York.
PENGUIN and PENGUIN WORKSHOP are trademarks of Penguin Books Ltd.
WHO HQ & Design is a registered trademark of Penguin Random House LLC.
Printed in the USA.

Visit us online at www.penguinrandomhouse.com.

Library of Congress Control Number: 2017010011

ISBN 9780448489193 (paperback) 10 9 8
ISBN 9780515157970 (library binding) 10 9 8 7 6 5 4 3 2

Contents

Who Was Bob Marley? 1
The Country Boy 7
Another Side of Jamaica 18
From Welder to Wailer 28
Love and Success 40
The Path to Stardom 55
56 Hope Road 72
The Fight for Peace 81
A Legend and His Legacy 96
Timelines 106
Bibliography 108

Who Was Bob Marley?

When he was twelve years old, Bob Marley and his mother, Cedella, boarded the bungo-bungo. That was what people in the Jamaican countryside called the public buses. Bob and Cedella were riding from their small, friendly village, called Nine Mile, to Kingston, Jamaica's capital city.

Watching their neighbors wave good-bye, Cedella wasn't as sad as Bob. He was probably thinking about what they were leaving behind: soccer games in the grassy hills and the music his neighbors played on their porches at night. But Cedella was sure she could find a better life for herself and her son in Kingston.

So in 1957, Bob and Cedella rolled down Jamaica's dirt roads in the bungo-bungo to their new home.

They moved to a Kingston neighborhood called Trench Town. When they arrived, Bob was nervous about what he saw.

Trench Town was a part of the city with run-down buildings and streets crowded with people who were very poor. Many called it a slum. There was no indoor plumbing, so the people of Trench Town had to collect water from pumps in public spaces, called yards. Public yards were like dusty parks set in the middle of big concrete apartment buildings that had been built by the government.

Trench Town could be a dangerous place. People sometimes stole from one another and fought in the street. Bob kept to himself and observed his new neighborhood, trying hard to feel at home there.

Bob noticed that the public yards were where neighbors gathered to talk or play cards and soccer. Some kids played music there. Sometimes it could seem almost like Nine Mile!

When Bob played his guitar in the yard by his house, other kids noticed how talented he was. They even asked to play with him.

Singing and playing with his new neighbors in the public yard, Bob celebrated the good things in life, like having a full meal and a close friend. It seemed the struggles of the poorest people in Kingston made them appreciate the joy that music brought to their lives more than anyone Bob had ever met.

That's when Bob knew he always wanted to make music—the kind that brought people together to share simple, everyday joys. And Bob went on to do just that. His music continues to inspire and uplift people everywhere.

CHAPTER 1
The Country Boy

By the time Robert Nesta Marley was born in 1945, the island country of Jamaica had been ruled by Great Britain for nearly three hundred years.

Bob's father, Norval Marley, was a white man who was employed by the British government. Norval's job was to manage government-owned property in the village of Nine Mile in the district of Saint Ann Parish, Jamaica. A parish is another name for a county. Jamaica has fourteen parishes.

Norval was a little over sixty years old when he moved to a small shack in Nine Mile. He soon fell in love with Cedella Malcolm, a beautiful black Jamaican girl much younger than he was. Cedella's grandmother owned the shack where Norval lived. By the time Cedella was eighteen, she was married to Norval and expecting her first child.

Norval Marley

Neighbors did not approve of Cedella marrying a white man so much older than she was. Cedella wanted to build a better life for herself and hoped Norval would help her see the world beyond the Jamaican countryside.

But soon after the marriage, Norval had to leave Nine Mile. He said that working in the hills was not good for his health. He needed to find an easier job in Kingston. Norval promised Cedella he would return. Years later, he did, but only for a short time. They never lived together again.

Their baby, Robert Nesta Marley, was born in Nine Mile on February 6, 1945. From the start, Bob was a good boy. With his father gone, his grandfather taught him many things.

He explained Bible stories to Bob and taught him how to farm potatoes and yams. Bob's grandparents were always proud of how hard he worked—even when he was very young. Bob was a quick learner at everything he did. His teachers at school said he was ahead of the other kids in his class.

Sometime before he turned ten, Bob stepped on a piece of glass while playing soccer barefoot.

The cut on his toe became infected. Bob limped for a long time. Finally, Bob's cousin brought him some natural medicine that he had made from herbs. His foot healed, but it was never quite the same.

While he rested, Bob picked at a guitar that the same cousin had made for him out of bamboo and goatskin. He spent hours and hours with the guitar while his foot healed.

Folk Instruments of Jamaica

For much of the twentieth century, people in the Jamaican countryside made their musical instruments by hand. One of the most popular was the rumba box. A rumba box is usually made of wood, and it has a hole cut in the front like a guitar.

But unlike a guitar, a rumba box has small metal strips screwed in a straight line at the bottom of the hole. The metal strips are like keys on a piano. The rumba-box player sits on top of the box and reaches down to play the keys.

Other handmade instruments were the shake-shake (an instrument similar to maracas) and simple wood blocks knocked together to keep rhythm. Drums, banjos, and guitars were made out of buckets, bamboo, sardine cans, and cowhide or goatskin.

When Bob was still a young boy, Cedella opened her own grocery store. Thaddius "Toddy" Livingston owned a grocery in Nine Mile, too. Cedella and Toddy began spending a lot of time together, even though Toddy was married. Toddy also had a son Bob's age named Neville. His nickname was "Bunny."

Bunny and Bob went to the same school and worked at their families' grocery stores in the afternoons. They had something else in common: They both loved music! Bob and Bunny became close friends. They played their homemade guitars together at the end of the day when all their homework and chores were done.

Bob began music lessons with his neighbor, Mrs. James. She taught him to play calypso—a type of folk music that originated in Trinidad and Tobago, another Caribbean island nation. Calypso is a style of music with a strong, recognizable beat. The words often reflect everyday life and island politics.

When Bob was twelve, Toddy decided a big city like Kingston would be better for business and for Bunny. The Livingstons were moving away from Nine Mile.

Cedella agreed with Toddy. Before long, she and Bob were on a bus winding down the mountains to a new life in Kingston, too.

CHAPTER 2
Another Side of Jamaica

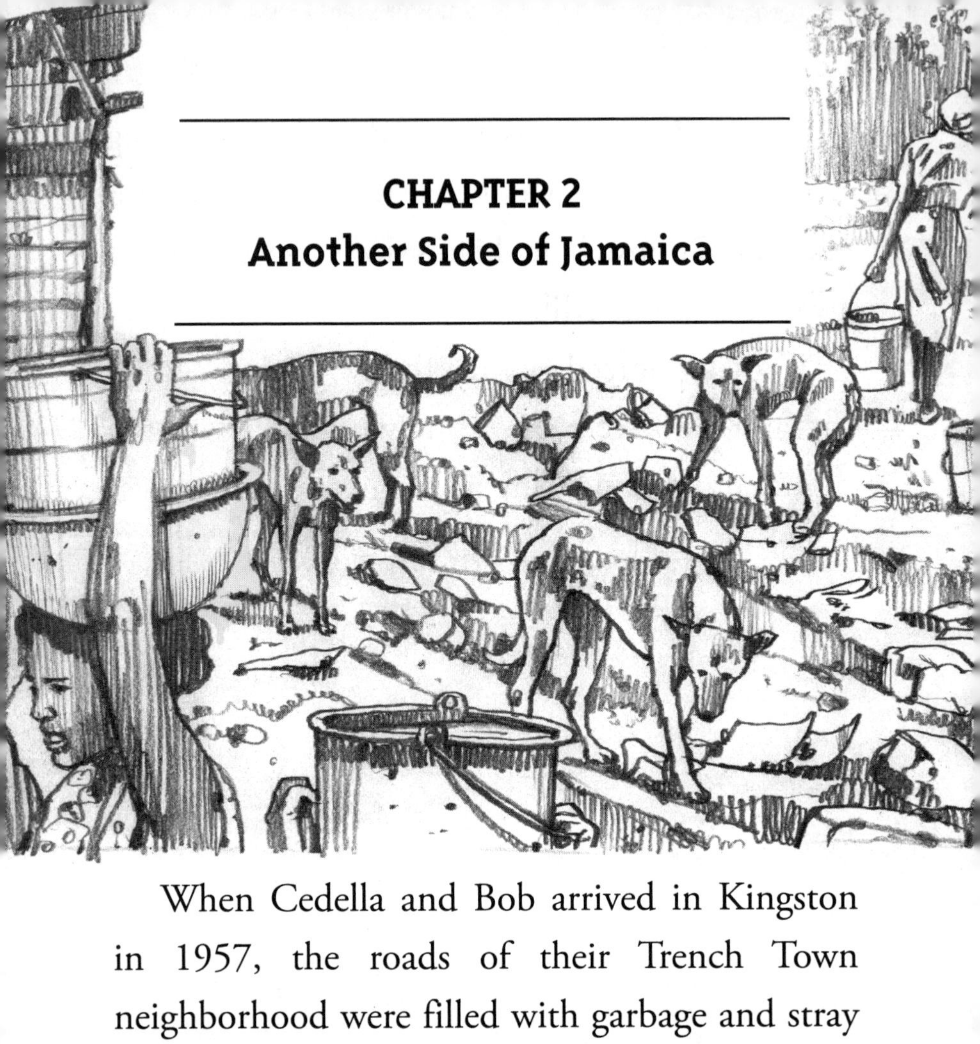

When Cedella and Bob arrived in Kingston in 1957, the roads of their Trench Town neighborhood were filled with garbage and stray dogs. There was no sewage system, so people went to the bathroom outside in holes dug in the dirt. People pumped water for drinking, cooking, and bathing from an outdoor well.

The children in the neighborhood knew Bob was from a country village. He also didn't look like the other kids in Trench Town. He had lighter skin because his father was white. He was always teased because he was mixed race: both black and white. Bob had to learn how to defend himself against other boys.

Bob quickly learned how to fight. The neighborhood boys thought he knew some pretty quick martial-arts moves. He didn't, but he still earned the nickname "Tuff Gong": *Tuff* because he seemed so tough, and *Gong* because the kids were reminded of the loud instrument from kung-fu movies when they saw Bob fight. Bob's physical skill became known around Trench Town.

Bob wouldn't have had to fight so much if he had been going to school. But in Jamaica, only elementary school was free. After that, you had to pay to attend. Cedella didn't have the money to send Bob right away. While she was working hard to save up, Bob missed a year of school. He spent his days working any job he could to help his mother pay for food and rent.

Cedella and Toddy were still spending much of their time together. Eventually, Bob and Cedella moved into the Livingstons' house on Second Street. Bob was glad that he would now be living with his friend Bunny.

Bob and Bunny listened to music on the radio all the time. American singers and musicians like Sam Cooke, Fats Domino, and Ray Charles became Bob's heroes. Bob and Bunny tried to copy the biggest radio hits on their guitars.

Bob and Bunny began writing their first songs together. Bob combined his favorite calypso beats with the American music he heard on Kingston radio. They played them in the Second Street public yard, and people liked them.

In 1959, when Bob was about fourteen, Cedella had finally saved enough money to send him to school. She had worked long hours to pay for his clothes and books. Bob's new teachers said he was thoughtful and smart. But Bob's time there wouldn't last long. The school closed a short time later, and Bob began looking for a new job instead of a new school.

Desmond Dekker

Desmond Dekker, a friend Bob had met playing music in the yards, worked at a Kingston welding business. Bob soon got a job there as well. He did not like the work. But he got to spend time with Desmond, who was a talented singer.

Desmond and Bob both listened to ska music. Ska is Jamaican music that has a regular rhythm like calypso but usually adds the sound of horns like trumpets, saxophones, and trombones.

People could really dance to it. There were plenty of ska songs on the radio at the time, and Desmond had written and sung some of them! One of his hits was called "King of Ska." Bob enjoyed making friends with talented people.

Joe Higgs was another famous musician in Trench Town. He lived one block away from Bob and Bunny. He organized jam sessions for musicians to meet up and play in one of the public yards every night.

One night, Joe noticed Bob and Bunny playing together. He saw how quickly Bob learned new things on the guitar and how well he could sing. It didn't matter that Bob's guitar was made from a sardine can—Bob was that good. Joe introduced himself, and the three became friends. They stayed up all night playing music under the stars.

"Joe Higgs 'elped me understand that music," Bob said, in his Jamaican accent. He was beginning to see that he would rather make music than do anything else.

CHAPTER 3
From Welder to Wailer

In 1961, not long after Bob started his job as a welder, he had an accident. While he was working, a small piece of metal flew into his eye! Bob had to go to the hospital and have the metal removed. It only took a little while to heal, but during that time Bob became surer than ever that he would rather work on his music than do anything else.

Bob spent all his free time with Joe Higgs and Bunny, playing music. When Bob was still only sixteen, Joe helped him record his first song. It was a song with a ska beat called "Judge Not." The words reflected what Bob's grandfather had taught him from the Bible:

Judge not,
If you're not ready for judgment.

Bob wanted people to accept others, no matter how different they seemed to be.

"Judge Not" was played on the radio, but it wasn't a hit. People thought it was too much like the songs they heard in church. Bob was disappointed, but not for long. He knew he had so many more songs to record! He soon met someone else who was also hard at work writing songs.

One day, Bob and Bunny bumped right into a man who was playing his guitar and singing as he walked. His name was Peter McIntosh,

but he was called "Tosh." He had written the song he had been playing. Tosh was very tall, and like Bob, he had a reputation for being a bit tough. The three of them talked for a long time on the street and soon became friends.

Bob and Bunny introduced Tosh to Joe Higgs. The three friends played together in Joe's recording studio. Joe knew right away that they were a great team. And just like that, Bob was part of a band.

They called themselves "The Wailing Wailers." *Wail* means to cry. People said Bob sometimes sounded like he was crying when he sang. The Wailing Wailers wanted to write songs about how it felt to live in Trench Town.

Joe made sure they practiced every day and night, sometimes until around five in the morning. To see how people liked their new songs, the Wailing Wailers stood on street corners performing. Crowds of people in Trench

Town gathered and danced and sang along, just like they had in the yards. The Wailing Wailers were making a name for themselves.

They were becoming popular with the girls in Trench Town, too.

In 1962, Bob met a girl named Cheryl Murray. Cheryl's brother didn't like Bob, but they dated anyway. Cheryl became pregnant, and gave birth to Bob's first child, Imani Carole, on May 22, 1963. Cheryl's brother warned Bob to stay away from Imani. Bob didn't want any trouble, so he did.

That same year, Cedella and Toddy had a daughter. Her name was Claudette "Pearl" Livingston.

In addition to the new baby, there was much excitement throughout the country. Jamaica had become independent from Britain! The country celebrated, including the residents of Trench Town. A new sewage system to deliver water was built there almost right away.

But Bob could only celebrate for so long. He was eighteen years old, and many things in his life were changing. Cedella realized she hadn't found the life she wanted in Kingston. She decided to move to the United States. Bob's mother and baby Pearl went to live with relatives in Wilmington, Delaware. Bob stayed behind in Trench Town, living at Toddy's house. He began to feel unwelcome. So Bob often stayed at other friends' homes.

When Bob didn't have a place to stay, he slept outside in the public yards. Bob often saw a homeless Rastafarian named Georgie there. A lot of people Bob knew were Rastafari (say: ras-ta-FAR-eye), including Joe Higgs.

Bob and Georgie would sometimes talk all night when Bob wasn't busy playing or writing songs. Bob respected Georgie. His thoughts were similar to Bob's understanding of what he had read in the Bible. During those nights cooking and sleeping in the yard, Georgie explained his Rastafari beliefs to Bob. Soon, the Rasta way of life would inspire Bob and his music like nothing else ever had.

Rastafari

Haile Selassie I coronation

In 1930, a man named Ras Tafari Makonnen was crowned emperor of Ethiopia. He took the royal name of Haile Selassie I. Some people believed Emperor Selassie was God. They called themselves Rastafari in his honor. Rastafarians—or Rastas—

believe that the families of former slaves will one day be led back to Africa by God, whom they call Jah.

Rastas believe the body is an important part of spirituality. They exercise regularly and eat healthy food. Most are vegetarian or vegan. Rastas believe in peaceful attitudes toward all people, animals, plants, and other living things. They smoke ganja (say: GAN-ja)—marijuana—which is an herb that they believe increases their spiritual awareness.

Rastas are forbidden to cut their hair because hair is considered a source of power and inner strength. They often wear their hair in long dreadlocks.

Today, about one million people practice Rastafari worldwide.

CHAPTER 4
Love and Success

Coxsone Dodd

By 1964, Bob, Bunny, and Tosh were known in Trench Town simply as the Wailers. But there was one very important person who hadn't met them yet. His name was Coxsone Dodd.

Coxsone Dodd was famous in Jamaica. He produced nearly all the hit songs that played on the radio. He was also the founder of Studio One, the first black-owned recording studio in Jamaica. Studio One was on Greenwich Park Road, just a few blocks from Bunny's house.

One day, Bob and the band heard some very good news: Coxsone was holding auditions for new bands at Studio One every Sunday. So in the summer of 1964, the Wailers went to audition.

When the band arrived, they were led to the backyard of the studio. Under a mango tree, the Wailers played five songs. The last song they played was called "Simmer Down." Bob wrote "Simmer Down" as a warning against street violence:

Simmer down, oh, control your temper
Simmer down, for the battle will be hotter . . .

Coxsone stopped the band before they could finish their last song. "Okay, that one: Come tomorrow and we'll record that one," Coxsone said. So they did!

Coxsone made sure the song was played on the radio. People loved it! Everyone in Kingston knew about the dangers of Trench Town. Listeners understood the warning in the song. The recording of "Simmer Down" sold nearly eighty thousand copies!

The Wailers spent the rest of 1964 at Studio One recording their first album. Because Bob still didn't have a home of his own, Coxsone let him sleep there, too.

Coxsone became like a father to Bob. When days were hard, he reminded him, "Now, young man, be strong. Think. You can make music. Write. Sing." He helped Bob stay focused on his music and kept him from getting discouraged.

Many of Coxsone's friends were Rastafarians. They shared their thoughts about the world and their spiritual beliefs with Bob. Bob agreed with their ideas about peace and justice, but he carefully considered what he was told. Would he give up the Christian faith he had learned as a child?

Bob often walked the streets thinking about new songs he was eager to record. But one day, someone distracted him. A young woman named Rita Anderson lived down the street from Studio One, on Greenwich Park Road. Rita was a local girl with a great voice. Bob watched Rita singing in her window as he walked by. Rita saw Bob, too.

Rita was the single mother of a little girl named Sharon. One Sunday afternoon, Rita worked up the nerve to audition for Coxsone Dodd. Coxsone liked Rita enough to ask her to return to Studio One and sing again. Bob finally got to meet her, and he didn't waste any time. He invited Rita and a couple of her friends to be backup singers on the new album. The girls called themselves the Soulettes.

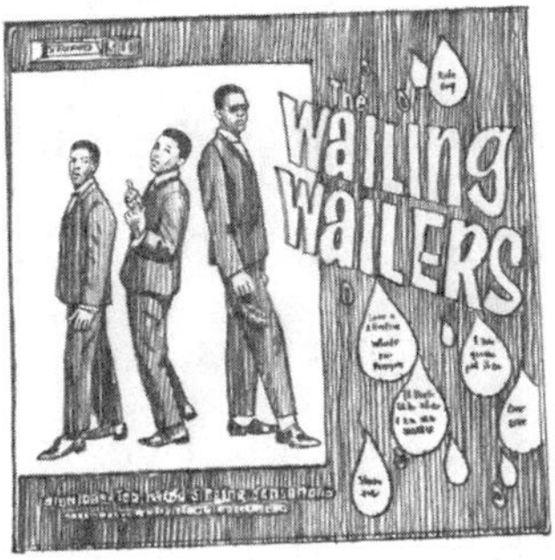

By the end of 1964, the Wailers finished their first album, called simply *The Wailing Wailers*. Bob was only nineteen years old.

Bob, Bunny, Tosh, Rita, and the rest of the band went on tour throughout the country to perform their new songs. Some of their songs were love songs. Others told true stories about their rough life in Kingston. It was one of the first times Jamaicans could hear songs about the struggles of their everyday lives played on the radio.

Many Jamaicans felt like the Wailers were old friends and neighbors. The album was a big hit, first in Trench Town, then all over Jamaica.

The band toured Jamaica for a couple of years. Rita and Bob fell in love. Bob helped Rita take care of her young daughter, Sharon, when the tour was over. On February 10, 1966, Rita and Bob got married. It was only four days after Bob's twenty-first birthday. Rita was just a year younger.

They celebrated with a traditional Jamaican wedding meal of curried goat, rice, and green bananas. Rita's auntie cooked the food, even though she was nervous about the marriage. She worried that Bob wouldn't want to settle down. Even though Bob loved Rita very much, he had a lot of big dreams about playing his music. It turned out Rita's auntie was right: The very night of their wedding, Bob and the Wailers were scheduled to play their biggest concert yet at Kingston's National Stadium!

Bob's mother didn't know about his marriage to Rita. She had already arranged for him to join her in Delaware. So just two days after his wedding, Bob flew to the United States for the first time. Rita was sad. But she understood that Bob could make more money working in the US.

When Bob arrived in Delaware, he went to work right away. First, he worked at Chrysler Motors building cars. Next, he took a job at the Hotel DuPont in Wilmington vacuuming carpets. At the end of his workday, Bob strummed his guitar and wrote songs.

In the meantime, Coxsone released some of the songs the Wailers had recorded earlier. The band continued to play shows with Bunny singing Bob's parts. Bob wasn't too mad about it. After all, he didn't want Jamaicans to forget about the Wailers.

The Wailers weren't the only people who were becoming more popular in Jamaica. By the 1960s, many Jamaicans had become Rastafarians. When Emperor Haile Selassie I of Ethiopia visited Jamaica in 1966, one hundred thousand people greeted him as he exited his plane at the Kingston airport!

Haile Selassie I (1892–1975)

Born Ras Tafari Makonnen, Haile Selassie I was the emperor of Ethiopia from 1930 to 1974. He was an Orthodox Christian who was given the name Haile Selassie I (say: HIGH-lay si-LAH-si) at his baptism. As a member of the royal line of Ethiopian rulers, part of his long official title was

"the Conquering Lion of Judah"—which many Rastafarians understood to mean that he was a living god. The Lion of Judah is an important Rasta image that has come to symbolize Selassie.

Back in the US, Bob was disappointed. His belief in the Rastafari faith had become stronger while the band had toured the countryside of Jamaica. Many Jamaicans believed that Emperor Selassie was a living version of God, and Bob wanted to be there to greet him. In a letter to Rita, he wrote, "Go and see [him] for yourself." Rita was unsure about Selassie, but she went anyway.

Rita had an experience she didn't expect. She wrote to Bob afterward, "I looked into his hand, and there was the nail-print." Rita was talking about the part in the Bible when Jesus is nailed to a cross through his hands. After seeing Haile Selassie I's hand as he waved from his car,

Rita was convinced that Selassie *was* God. She wrote that Rastafari beliefs were "the same as Christianity, but with maybe a little more freedom."

Bob was happy for her. And he was ready to go home. He wanted to be with his wife and to record all the songs he had been writing during his lonely nights in the States. After eight long months, Bob gladly returned to Jamaica. He was ready to return to his music as well.

CHAPTER 5
The Path to Stardom

At the end of 1966, Bob and Rita settled into her small house on Greenwich Park Road. Finally, they lived together as husband and wife.

While Bob had been in the US, he had stopped cutting his hair, in keeping with his Rasta beliefs. As Bob walked the streets of Trench Town again, he noticed that many people were growing their hair out, too. He and other Jamaicans now had long hair that naturally separated into sections. These sections were the beginning of dreadlocks—created by twisting pieces of hair together so they grow out to look like thin ropes.

Something else was new in Jamaica: A popular style of music called rocksteady was playing on the radio. It is slower than ska and has a more relaxed beat. Like calypso, the words to rocksteady songs can be very political.

Bob really liked the new music. It inspired him to go back to Studio One and play with the Wailers. Together with Coxsone, they created what is now called reggae (say: REH-gay). Reggae music combines calypso, rocksteady, and other Jamaican music styles with American pop music. But it has a beat that is all its own.

Many reggae songs were about Rastafarian concerns, like poverty, justice, politics, and Africa. Reggae became known as music for people who had been oppressed—or kept under the power of a greater authority. Jamaicans knew about oppression from the years they had been under British rule. Reggae quickly became a part of Rastafarian and Jamaican culture, also known as roots culture. The term "roots" refers to the spirituality and pride of a black culture that has its source—its roots—in Africa.

With a lot of new songs in his notebook, Bob was ready to record a new album. But he wanted to be his own boss. Bob wanted to save enough money to make the next album without Coxsone.

During the late 1960s, when the Wailers' career was just beginning, people listened to music on the radio or by playing vinyl (plastic) records on turntables. Bob and Rita decided to record songs one at a time, whenever they could afford to rent a recording studio. They sold the new records—single songs only—from their bedroom window, which they had turned into a small storefront. They called it the Wail'n Soul'm store, named after the Wailers and the Soulettes.

Bob and Rita were happy to be selling records together. They were a great team.

On August 23, 1967, they had their first child. They named their daughter Cedella, after Bob's mother.

Just over a year later, Rita gave birth to a baby boy. "This first son . . . What shall we call him?" Rita wondered. Bob noticed that the baby's foot was turned in a little. "Well, this is Ziggy!" he said.

Ziggy was Bob's nickname on the soccer field because he ran and changed direction so fast. So they named him David "Ziggy" Marley.

Bob and Rita had finally saved enough money to record a whole new album. The Wailers were ready to go back to work. But they needed a place to record.

Luckily, they made a new friend in Kingston who had his own recording studio. His name was Lee "Scratch" Perry. Scratch was a good match for Bob. He wanted the band to follow their dreams and make reggae music in their own style.

Lee "Scratch" Perry

As the Wailers recorded the album, daily politics in Jamaica gave Bob more ideas for songs. Two political parties fought for power in the island nation: the Jamaica Labour Party (JLP) and the People's National Party (PNP). Violent gunfights often broke out in the streets between members of the JLP and the PNP. Both wanted to control Jamaica.

The fighting reminded Bob of the roughness in the public yards. He wanted to record songs that would bring people together. He believed in peace. In the song "Fussing and Fighting," Bob sang:

We should really love each other
In peace and harmony

No matter which part of the island they were from, Jamaican people were comforted by the band's peaceful message. And the band's popularity was growing outside the country as well. Scratch had friends in London who really liked the Wailers' music. Soon, their songs were being played on the radio in the United Kingdom (the UK) and even in the US.

By 1971, Bob Marley and the Wailers had made two new albums with Scratch, *Soul Rebel* and *Soul Revolution*. They toured in Jamaica, the UK, and the US.

While he was in England, Bob heard about

a man named Chris Blackwell. Chris was from Jamaica, and he was a big fan of Bob's music. He was also the founder of Island Records, a very successful international record label.

When they finally met, Chris was impressed with the Wailers. He said, "From the day I met them, I saw something about them that was different from ordinary Trench Town bad boys—there was some class to them, some future." So the Wailers decided to work with Chris and record on Island Records.

Chris, Bob, and the Wailers made two new albums in 1972 and 1973: *Catch A Fire* and *Burnin'*. Chris booked concerts and made sure the Wailers' music was played on the radio in Jamaica and the UK. Bob and the Wailers were becoming famous for their reggae music.

In the 1970s, wars were happening throughout the world. In addition to the Vietnam War, there were conflicts in the African nations of Angola and Sudan, and in the Central American countries of Guatemala and Nicaragua. People were suffering in many different countries.

The Wailers' song "Get Up, Stand Up" had an important message to people all over the world. The lyrics said:

Get up, stand up: Stand up for your rights.
Get up, stand up: Don't give up the fight!

Like so many of Bob's songs, it was about the justice, peace, and unity that people wanted to see in their lives. It was music that gave people hope that things could change for the better.

While they were touring the world, Bob and the Wailers had become especially popular in

England. In 1975, Bob and the Wailers gave concerts at the Lyceum Ballroom in London. Both shows, on July 17 and 18, were sold out. Three thousand more fans without tickets struggled to get inside.

CEUM
LYCEUM THEATRE

Bob and the Wailers played their most popular songs that night. One of them was called "No Woman, No Cry." In the song, Bob sang about Georgie and the Trench Town yards. He repeats the line "Everything's gonna be all right!" And people believed him. One fan said, "Every person who was there decided they were a Rasta." Bob had become a spiritual leader.

The band was launched to superstardom. And Bob Marley became known as the "King of Reggae."

CHAPTER 6
56 Hope Road

By the mid-1970s, the Wailers were big stars. Songs from their two Island Records albums climbed the charts in the UK and the US. As a way to congratulate the band and show them he wanted to help them record more albums, Chris gave them a home he owned at 56 Hope Road.

56 Hope Road was a big white house in a wealthy neighborhood of Kingston. It became a hangout for friends of the band. Any hour of the night or day, musicians came and went. They wrote songs, played soccer, shared a meal, and talked about their Rastafari faith.

By this time, Bob lived strictly by the Rasta way of life. He woke up early every morning to run. He kept a strict vegetarian diet, never eating any meat. He also studied the Bible the way Rastas understood it. Parts of the house at 56 Hope Road were even painted the colors of the Ethiopian flag. Bob was on a mission to carry the Rasta message of harmony and goodwill to the world.

56 Hope Road was a great place for Bob to work and relax. The trouble was that his family had no place there. There was always noise and ganja smoke in the air. So Bob's family lived in an apartment far from Hope Road. Bob visited them sometimes, and Rita and the children visited him, too.

Green, Gold, and Red

The flag of Ethiopia is an important Rastafarian symbol to those who live in Jamaica and other countries around the world. The green, gold, and red stripes of the flag have become symbolic colors of love and loyalty throughout the Rasta community.

While on tour, Bob had children with women other than Rita. He had two sons born in 1972 to different mothers. Rita also had their second son, Stephen, in 1972. The next year, Bob had a new daughter born in England to yet another mother. Bob eventually had thirteen children, some adopted, with eight different mothers.

This was not easy for Rita. Soon, there was a rumor that Rita was dating another man. In 1974, she had her last child, Stephanie. Bob adopted Stephanie, but she wasn't his child. Through it all, Rita and Bob stayed married.

Meanwhile, people were becoming very anxious about the political parties in Jamaica, as the JLP and the PNP fought for control.

Some Jamaican citizens began working hard to elect one party or the other. This led to arguments over which party could provide more jobs, because most people in Jamaica were still very poor. The arguments turned violent, and many street gangs were formed. Suddenly it seemed as if everyone had guns.

Bob had a lot of influence in Jamaica. Politicians knew he could get people to vote a certain way just by saying he liked one party better than the other. An old friend of his explained in that familiar Jamaican accent, "Everyone want Bob Marley [on] their team." But Bob didn't want to get involved in politics. Just like when he was younger, Bob only fought when he had to. But he couldn't stop the fighting from showing up at his own door.

On December 3, 1976, a group of men with guns approached the back door of 56 Hope Road.

They began to fire shots into the kitchen, where Bob stood with his cook. Rita and the children were visiting Bob at the time. As Rita drove away, a bullet grazed the back of her head. Bob was shot in the upper arm. Everyone survived.

But they realized that Jamaica's political violence was reaching far beyond the slums of Trench Town.

To be safe, Bob flew back to England. Rita and the children remained in Kingston. But they stayed far away from the trouble at 56 Hope Road.

CHAPTER 7
The Fight for Peace

Bob was glad to be in England. The attack at his home made him feel certain that it was important to work for peace in Jamaica and throughout the world. Bob thought his music could inspire that peace.

By 1976, Bob was an international star and role model. That year, Bob Marley and the Wailers were named "Band of the Year" by *Rolling Stone* magazine. Bob was featured on the cover. People all over the world admired him.

But before Bob could make a new record, Bunny and Tosh left the Wailers. They wanted to make their own albums. Bob organized a new band and made two very popular albums with Chris Blackwell: *Rastaman Vibration* in 1976 and *Exodus* in 1977. In May 1977, Bob and his new band, now called "Bob Marley and the Wailers," flew to Paris to begin their new tour.

On the day before the first show, the band relaxed by playing a game of soccer. During the game, someone stepped hard on Bob's toe by accident. It was the same toe that had been infected when he was a young boy.

Bob was in pain, but he didn't let anyone know it. He and the band went on to play that night. One of the reviewers from the show in Paris wrote, "[Bob's] energy and surprisingly inventive dancing was a joyful sight. . . . Arms and dreadlocks flailing, he was a magical picture."

While Bob traveled on tour with the band, he didn't complain. But he changed the bandages on his foot a lot. Sometimes, he found his boot was full of blood.

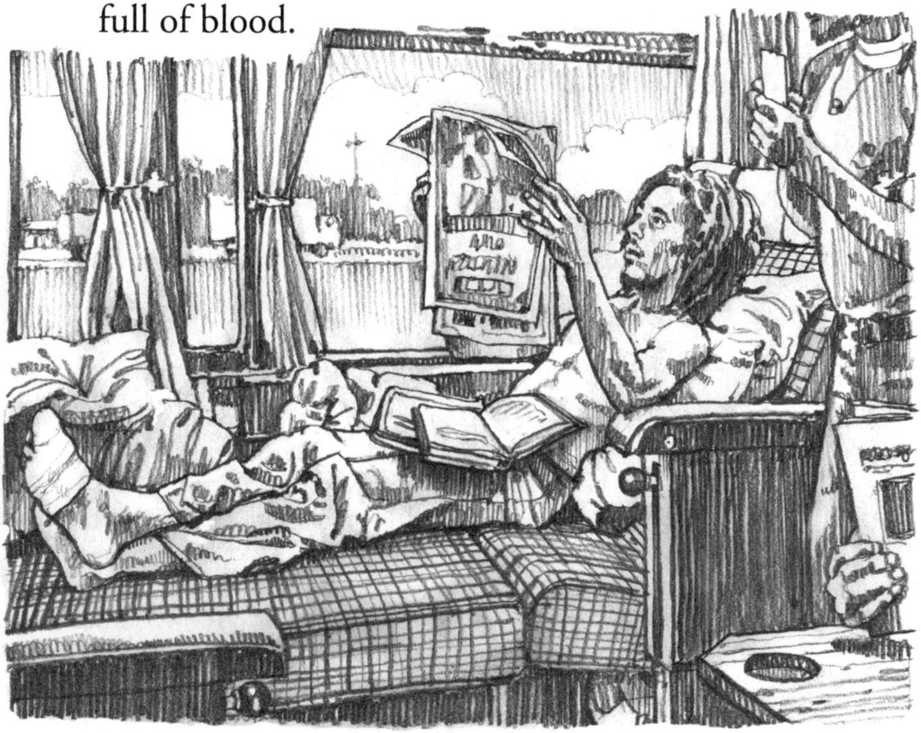

By the end of the European tour, Bob could no longer walk. Finally, he went to sec a doctor in London. Everyone was shocked by the news he received.

Bob had a very serious form of skin cancer. Some people wondered if the childhood infection Bob had on his toe had caused the cancer. The doctor told him he had to choose: "the toe or the tour." He advised Bob to have his toe cut off to stop the spread of the cancer.

The US tour for *Exodus* was canceled. Bob had surgery to remove the cancer, but not the entire toe. He was afraid he wouldn't be able to play soccer or dance again. After the surgery, Bob stayed with his mother at her new home in Miami, Florida.

It was a warm place for him to heal. But Bob didn't always see his doctor for checkups, as he was supposed to.

After a few months, Bob felt strong again. He returned to Jamaica for the first time in nearly a year and a half. He decided to help organize the One Love Peace Concert in Kingston. It would be a chance for all of Jamaica to come together. Bob still hoped that music could unite his beloved homeland. The concert was named for Bob's song "One Love," which repeats these words:

One Love!

One Heart!

Let's get together and feel all right!

On April 22, 1978, over thirty thousand people attended the concert at the National Stadium in Kingston! Sixteen Jamaican reggae bands played. Bob also invited two very special guests: Michael Manley, the cofounder of the PNP, and Edward Seaga, the leader of the JLP.

Bob sang "Jammin'" for the audience. It was a song about finding the strength to overcome life's struggles. Bob was preaching the same lessons he had in his very first song, "Judge Not." But now people listened. And they loved the message.

While the band continued playing, Bob stopped singing for a moment.

He asked Michael Manley and Edward Seaga to join him onstage. "I just want to shake hands and show the people that we're gonna unite," Bob said. He took the men's hands and held them over his head. Bob wanted to fill his country with the hope that peace was possible.

The concert didn't solve Jamaica's problems. But on June 15, Bob was awarded the United Nations Peace Medal of the Third World in New York City. The award was given to him by African political leaders of the United Nations. Bob was beaming with pride that day—his heart filled with hope.

At the end of 1978, Bob went to Africa for the first time. He visited Ethiopia, the spiritual home of all Rastafari. Emperor Selassie had died a few years earlier, in 1975, so Bob never got the chance to meet him. But it was still a very important experience for him.

Just over a year later, Bob was asked to perform in Zimbabwe for a very special celebration. On April 18, 1980, Zimbabwe declared its independence from Britain just like Jamaica had almost twenty years earlier. Bob was overjoyed to be a part of an African nation's independence.

But instead of the people of Zimbabwe, only powerful government leaders and its wealthiest citizens were in the audience. Bob and the band began to play, though they were disappointed at the situation. The people of Zimbabwe didn't like it, either.

Suddenly, riots broke out.

VIVA
ZIMBABWE
INDEPENDENCE 18th APRIL 1980

The crowd outside broke into the stadium. Bob was temporarily blinded by tear gas. Fighting began below the stage and turned violent. People fought security guards with anything they could find.

Bob was terribly sad. The riots reminded him of all the violence back home in Jamaica.

Again, Bob turned to music for peace. His experience in Zimbabwe inspired the album *Uprising*. His new songs were about unity, injustice, and the violence he had witnessed in Zimbabwe and throughout his life.

CHAPTER 8
A Legend and His Legacy

In June 1980, the album *Uprising* was released. The album was a hit in the UK and was rising up the US charts.

In September, Bob and the Wailers performed at Madison Square Garden in New York City. The shows were packed. Bob had reached a new level of success and had many fans in the US.

Sometimes, when Bob and Rita were in New York City, they went to church together on Sundays, especially the Ethiopian Orthodox Church. The morning after the shows at Madison Square Garden, Rita called Bob to invite him to go along with her.

Bob sounded strange on the phone.

"What happened? You didn't sleep last night?" Rita asked. Bob said he felt nauseous. Rita stopped by his room to check on him.

He seemed like he just needed rest, so Rita went to church without him.

To get some air, Bob went jogging in Central Park with a couple of friends. Before they got very far, Bob collapsed. His friends helped him to his feet. They took Bob to the hospital.

The cancer from years before had spread to Bob's brain. The doctors said Bob was very sick. But they advised him to continue performing until he couldn't anymore. Rita was worried. She wanted to believe that there was something else they could do for Bob.

A few nights later, Bob gave his last performance in Pittsburgh, Pennsylvania. For ninety minutes, the band played and the crowd cheered, and no one could tell Bob was sick. When the show ended, the audience called the band back onstage to play some more. It was as great a show as ever.

Bob's doctors told him that he had only

three weeks left to live. But he was going to fight. Bob and his family traveled to Germany. There Bob received chemotherapy, a strong treatment for cancer that makes the body very weak.

Bob had always been thin. But the chemotherapy had made him skinny. He lost his hair. His dreadlocks had always been an important link to his Rastafari beliefs. Then, in a move that surprised his fans, Bob was baptized in the Orthodox Christian Church.

On February 6, 1981, Bob celebrated his thirty-sixth birthday in the hospital with friends and family. He wanted to travel back to Jamaica one last time. He had also just received the Jamaican Order of Merit, an honor reserved for two people each year. He left Germany and traveled to Florida so that he could see his mother.

On May 11, 1981, Bob died at a hospital in Miami with family by his side. He didn't live long enough to see Jamaica again.

Three days later, one hundred thousand people passed by Bob's coffin in Kingston to have their last look at the reggae superstar—as many people as had greeted Emperor Selassie years earlier. The Jamaican government paid for Bob's funeral.

And on May 21, he was buried with his guitar on the tallest hill in his hometown of Nine Mile.

In 1984, the album *Legend* was released. It is a collection of Bob's greatest hits. It is the top-selling reggae album of all time, and continues to sell thousands of copies each week. In fact, the album's strong, continuous sales have made it the second-longest-charting album in *Billboard* magazine's history.

Legend is really the only word to describe Bob Marley. In 1990, Jamaica declared Bob's birthday, February 6, Bob Marley Day. In 1994, he was inducted into the Rock and Roll Hall of Fame. Although he never received a Grammy while he was alive, Bob was awarded the Grammy Lifetime Achievement Award in 2001.

His creative family also continues his legacy. They write, sing, and produce music. Some design clothing, write books, and act. His children created 1Love, an organization that helps inspire people to "Get Up, Stand Up" and build a better world. They hope to carry on Bob's vision for global peace and love.

Bob once said, "I like to see mankind live together."

People of all races and religions still love Robert Nesta Marley for his message of hope. Across the world, they continue to be inspired by the man who promised "Every little thing gonna be all right."

Timeline of Bob Marley's Life

1945	Robert Nesta Marley is born on February 6
1957	Moves with his mother, Cedella, to Kingston, Jamaica
1962	Records his first single, "Judge Not"
1963	The Wailing Wailers are formed
1964	The Wailing Wailers' first single, "Simmer Down," is a number-one hit in Jamaica
1966	Marries Rita Anderson on February 10
1971	Signs a contract with Chris Blackwell of Island Records
1973	The Wailers release *Catch A Fire* in April
1975	Performs at the Lyceum Ballroom in London in July
1976	Bob is injured by gunfire at 56 Hope Road on December 3
1977	Bob is diagnosed with cancer
1978	One Love Peace Concert is held in Kingston, Jamaica, on April 22
	Bob is awarded the United Nations Peace Medal of the Third World on June 15
1980	Collapses while jogging in New York City on September 21
1981	Receives the Jamaican Order of Merit
	Dies from cancer on May 11 in Miami, Florida
1990	February 6, Bob's birthday, becomes Bob Marley Day in Jamaica

Timeline of the World

1945	World War II ends
	The United Nations is created
1947	India declares independence from Great Britain
1948	Apartheid (segregation) in South Africa begins
1949	The 45 rpm record—the vinyl single—is invented
1951	The color television is introduced
1953	Coronation of Queen Elizabeth II of the United Kingdom
1957	The Soviet Union launches *Sputnik*, the first man-made satellite
1960	John F. Kennedy is elected president of the United States
1962	Jamaica gains its independence from Great Britain
1963	Martin Luther King Jr. gives "I Have a Dream" speech in Washington, DC
1975	The Vietnam War ends
	First episode of the late-night TV comedy show *Saturday Night Live* airs
1976	The Apple Computer Company is formed on April 1 by Steve Jobs and Steve Wozniak
	The United States celebrates the two hundredth anniversary of the Declaration of Independence on July 4
1979	Margaret Thatcher becomes the first female prime minister of Great Britain
1981	IBM introduces the personal computer

Bibliography

*** Books for young readers**

Marley. Directed by Kevin Macdonald. New York: Magnolia Pictures, 2012.

*Marley, Cedella, and Gerald Hausman. ***The Boy from Nine Miles: The Early Life of Bob Marley***. Charlottesville, VA: Hampton Roads Publishing Company, 2002.

Marley, Rita, and Hettie Jones. ***No Woman No Cry: My Life with Bob Marley***. New York: Hyperion, 2004.

*Medina, Tony. ***I and I Bob Marley***. New York: Lee & Low Books, 2009.

Salewicz, Chris. ***Bob Marley: The Untold Story***. New York: Faber and Faber, 2009.

Taylor, Don, and Mike Henry. ***Marley and Me: The Real Bob Marley Story***. New York: Barricade Books, 1995.

Toynbee, Jason. ***Bob Marley: Herald of a Postcolonial World?*** Malden, MA: Polity Press, 2007.

White, Timothy. ***Catch a Fire: The Life of Bob Marley***. New York: Holt, Rinehart, and Winston, 1983.